APULEIUS: THE STORY OF CUPID AND PSYCHE

REGINE MAY

Apuleius: *The Story of Cupid and Psyche*

Translation, Introduction and Notes

by Regine May

For Amrita, my little butterfly

BLURB

The love story of Cupid and Psyche, the powerful god of love and a human girl, has fascinated readers for centuries, ever since it was written by the Roman author Apuleius in the second century AD. The enchanting story can be read as both the origin of many classic fairy tales like *Beauty and the Beast* or *Cinderella*, and as a philosophical portrait of the search of the human soul for the divine.

But first of all, it is a story about human nature, jealous mothers-in-law, talking birds, helpful friends, and the idea that love always wins in the end, even if that means facing bloodthirsty sheep or travelling to the Underworld and back.

This book offers a new translation of the Latin text into English, together with notes to explain the characters, historical and literary context, and some of Apuleius' learned allusions.

Dr Regine May is Associate Professor in Latin Language and Literature at the University of Leeds.

INTRODUCTION

Apuleius: the author and his times

Apuleius was born ca. 125 AD in Madauros in North Africa, which was a Roman province at the time. He spoke Latin and Greek, and possibly some native Northern African languages. After trips to Greece and what is now Turkey in his youth to study literature and philosophy, he spent his life in Carthage and Rome as a teacher of literature, rhetoric and public speaker. Little is known of his life, but in 158/159 AD he was put on trial for supposedly using magic and witchcraft to make his wife Pudentilla fall in love with him. We still have the speech in his self-defence, called *Apology*, or *Defence against the Accusation of Magic*. From that speech it is clear that Apuleius knows a lot about ancient magic, which was dangerous, because if he had been proven to be a magician, he might have been executed. We know that he must have been found innocent and released, because he managed to publish his defence speech afterwards. We also have some philosophical works and speeches written by him in the 160s, so it is clear that he survived the trial and its aftermath. He liked to see himself as a Platonic philosopher and public educator, giving speeches in Carthage to his adoring audience on topics as far apart as the nature of parrots from India, the weird habits of Greek philosophers, the fable of the fox and the crow, or the odd deaths of famous Greek writers. Other lost works he wrote ranged from hymns to Asclepius the god of healing to poems about toothpaste and books on trees and medicine – we have only a few sentences of these left.

His most important work is the *Metamorphoses*, also called *The Golden Ass*, which he probably wrote in the 170s or 180s AD. He probably died in Carthage in the 180s AD.

The *Metamorphoses* or *The Golden Ass*

The *Metamorphoses* in eleven books is the only complete Latin novel we have from the classical world. Its main character is Lucius, a young man from Corinth, who tells his story in his own voice of his travels through Greece on family business. When he gets to Thessaly, a part of Greece associated with witches in the ancient world, he finds out that his host's wife Pamphile and her maid Photis practice witchcraft. Driven by his curiosity, he befriends Photis and asks her to help him turn into a bird. She gets the potions wrong, and Lucius is accidentally transformed into a donkey. Photis quickly brings Lucius into the stable, and asks him to wait there until she can get the antidote: roses. She promises to find them for the donkey to eat on the next day, to turn him back into a human being. Lucius cannot talk any more, but still thinks and feels like a human. He is rather upset when in the middle of the night robbers break into the house and steal his host's money and himself as a beast of burden to carry their stolen goods away. Lucius and the robbers reach the cave where the robbers live, where Lucius hears them tell stories of their derring-do, which ironically all end with their robber captains' deaths.

Yet more robbers arrive and bring a prisoner along with them, the beautiful girl Charite, kidnapped by them on the evening of her marriage. To calm her down and cheer her up, the robbers' housekeeper, an old woman, tells Charite the story of Cupid and Psyche, which Lucius the donkey overhears, too. Afterwards, Charite tries to escape from the robbers by jumping on Lucius, but the robbers catch them. Just as the robbers want to kill her, a young man appears and persuades the robbers to make him their new leader because of his supposed daring deeds. Charite is very pleased to see him, as the young man is actually her fiancé, Tlepolemus, who has come to rescue her. Tlepolemus defeats the robbers and takes Charite home. Gratefully, they send the donkey to a life of asinine leisure in the countryside. Unfortunately, the slaves in charge of looking after Lucius treat him badly and are about to kill him just when a messenger arrives. He comes from the city where Tlepolemus and Charite lived, to announce their

terrible fate. Tlepolemus had been killed by a rival for
Charite's love, and she had herself taken bloody revenge on
her husband's murderer and killed herself afterwards.
Because their rightful masters are now dead, the slaves run
away, taking Lucius with them. Further misadventures
result in Lucius moving from owner to owner; he becomes
in turn the pack animal for some travelling priests for
whom he carries the statue of their goddess, a poor market
gardener, a cowardly Roman soldier, and two cooks for a
rich man.

During all this time, Lucius continues to overhear many
stories told to his owners and which he catches with his
massive donkey ears to satisfy his curiosity. Just like Cupid
and Psyche, these inset tales often reflect Lucius' own
situation or that of the people who are the audience of the
stories. Lucius, however, who is essentially naïve, curious
and not very bright, never realises this. Lucius' last owner,
the rich man Thiasus, is so impressed with the donkey's
ability to eat human food and drink wine during
banquets, that he wants to put him on public show in the
theatre in Corinth, alongside a woman who is condemned
to death by wild beasts for murdering five of her relatives.
Lucius is worried that the wild beasts might eat him
alongside the woman, and decides to run away from the
theatre. He escapes to the coast in Cenchreae the port of
Corinth, where he falls asleep. In the middle of the night
he prays to the Moon Goddess for help, and to his surprise
(and that of the reader!), the friendly and gentle goddess
Isis appears to him and tells him how to find the roses that

will turn him into a human being again. Lucius obeys her advice and eats the garlands held by a priest of Isis taking part in a religious procession for the goddess. Lucius turns back into a human being and becomes one of Isis' devoted followers. During the course of a year, Lucius undergoes several initiations into Isis' mystery cult and that of her divine consort Osiris, and moves to Rome, where he lives happily ever after as one of her priests.

Cupid and Psyche in the *Metamorphoses*

Cupid and Psyche forms the centre of the novel, and covers parts of three of its eleven books: the end of book 4, all of book 5, and most of book 6 (*Metamorphoses* 4.28-6.24); the numeration of the books and chapters is kept in this translation to make referencing and use of secondary literature easier for readers. The novel's hero Lucius overhears the story as it is told by the robbers' housekeeper to their captive Charite, but does not understand how the story in many ways is a reflection of his own experiences as man and donkey, which is typical of Lucius' lack of understanding of the world he inhabits, and of the role of the inset tales in the *Metamorphoses* themselves, of which *Cupid and Psyche* is the longest and most complex. Although different in gender, Psyche and Lucius share many life experiences: both have to travel far and wide through dangerous landscapes and are driven to act by their own innate curiosity, which leads them to misfortune. It was Lucius' curiosity that caused him to be transformed into a donkey, while Psyche is often described as curious and simple by the narrator, and her initial misfortune is caused by her ill-advised urge to discover Cupid's identity. When she opens Persephone's container out of curiosity and desire to look pretty, she collapses and needs to be rescued by Cupid, just as Lucius needs to be rescued and turned human again by the goddess Isis. Although Cupid suggests to his pregnant wife that their child will be a boy, it is in fact a girl, Pleasure, who is born, which makes the ending somewhat ambiguous. In just the same way, Lucius' fate has been seen by some scholars as less than straightforward: he is ordered to undergo multiple expensive initiations into various aspects of the Isis mysteries, feels he may have been financially exploited by some of Isis' and Osiris' priests.

Nevertheless, the story of *Cupid and Psyche* can be read, and in the eighteen hundred years of its existence, has many times, been read as a standalone tale, as a touching love story between the god of love and a human girl. Since the name 'Psyche' means both 'butterfly' and 'soul' in Greek, many scholars have read the tale as an allegory, a story with a hidden meaning, that of the human soul's search for divine love. In artistic images over the centuries, Psyche is often portrayed as a beautiful girl with butterfly wings, paired up with Cupid as a young man with bird wings. In Apuleius' tale, Cupid does indeed have these wings, but Psyche is a mere mortal girl who becomes a goddess at the very end of the story, without ever once having had any wings.

A playful tale

Although some statues and images of a young couple with bird and butterfly wings can be found in Greece and Rome before Apuleius' time, the story as we have it is almost certainly Apuleius' own invention. As a learned philosopher and educated teacher of literature, he turns the simple story of the love between god and human into a beautiful tale full of echoes of and allusions to other literature. The notes point out a few examples of this. For fuller accounts see the commentaries by Kennedy (1990) and Zimmerman et al (2004), and the other books listed in the bibliography below. Many of these allusions are humorous, since Apuleius gently plays with elevated classical texts by having his characters experience recognisably similar situations, but in a much more humble context.

Most important for readers through the ages were Apuleius' allusions to the Greek philosopher Plato (ca. 428-348 BC), for example when Psyche hanging on to Cupid's feet in *Met.* 5.24 seems to enact Plato's description in his dialogue *Phaedrus* of the human soul made heavy by forgetfulness and unable to pursue the divine. Other allusions are to Greek and Latin epic, texts that every ancient reader would have known intimately from school age onwards. For example, just like Odysseus in Homer's *Odyssey*, or Aeneas in Vergil's *Aeneid*, Psyche is pursued by a vengeful goddess. Again, these allusions are tongue in cheek: whereas the goddess Juno, for example, hounds Aeneas because they were on opposite sides during the Trojan War, Venus chases down Psyche because she is jealous of the girl's beauty. Further epic allusions are noted in the comments.

Tragedy and comedy are played with, too, in Apuleius' story: Psyche's dilemma when she thinks about stabbing the unknown monster, for example, echoes the indecisions of tragic heroines who need to decide how to act (for example, Medea debates with herself whether to kill her children or not), and the happy outcome of the story, a marriage between formerly socially unequal lovers, is that of many Greek and Roman comedies.

This kind of literary texture and playfulness can be found in the whole of the *Metamorphoses* and some of Apuleius' other works, but in *Cupid and Psyche* especially it adds to the pleasure felt by anyone who reads this ancient tale with some knowledge of other Greek or Latin literature. The notes help to track down some of Apuleius' allusions, but the story can also be enjoyed without this literary underpinning, just as a beautiful love story.

Language and style

Apuleius' language is extraordinary. His choice of words ranges from the very rude to the highly literary and refined, which the translation tries to imitate where possible. He likes repetitions and parallelisms, and his language is full of poeticisms and old words not found in Latin language for hundreds of years before he uses them again. To understand this kind of diverse style, one could imagine the effect a modern novel sprinkled with words and images from Shakespeare or Charles Dickens might have on its readers. This however does not make Apuleius' Latin difficult to read, on the contrary: his syntax is much easier for learners of Latin to master than that of Cicero, even though the words may form a challenge for smaller dictionaries. Still, Apuleius is a joy to read, both for the imaginative story and his charming language, and the tale of *Cupid and Psyche* especially has been read with pleasure by millions.

The translation is close to the Latin original text and, unlike many other adaptations, does not avoid potentially problematic topics such as Psyche's pregnancy and the graphic deaths of her sisters. The notes explain the nature of the characters and gods, unpack some allusions which may help to understand the story's literary texture and humour better, and give some idea of the historical or religious context of the narrative. Following Apuleius' practice, the translation gives the Latin names of the gods, but their often better known Greek names are given in the footnotes, too. A rough map at the back shows some of the places mentioned in the story.

Short bibliography

There are many books about Apuleius available, especially in recent years, and every year scholars add to the list. This short bibliography is only intended to give some basic information, but any readers wishing to explore the story of Cupid and Psyche in more detail could contact Regine May via email r.may@leeds.ac.uk or twitter @RegineMay.

https://ahc.leeds.ac.uk/languages/staff/92/dr-regine-may

Finkelpearl, E. (1998), *Metamorphosis of Language in Apuleius. A Study of Allusion in the Novel*, Ann Arbor.

Graverini, L. (2007), *Literature and Identity in the Golden Ass of Apuleius*, Columbus.

Harrison, S.J. (2000), *Apuleius. A Latin Sophist*, Oxford.

Harrison, S.J. (2013), *Framing The Ass. Literary Texture in Apuleius' Metamorphoses*, Oxford.

Hijmans, B.L. Jr. and van der Paardt, R.Th., eds. (1978), *Aspects of Apuleius' Golden Ass*, Groningen.

Kenney, E.J. (1990), *Apuleius Cupid and Psyche*, Cambridge.

May, R. (2006), *Apuleius and Drama. The Ass on Stage*, Oxford.

May, R. (2013), *Apuleius Metamorphoses or The Golden Ass. Book 1. With an Introduction, Translation and Notes*, Oxford.

Shumate, N.C. (1996), *Crisis and Conversion in Apuleius' Metamorphoses*, Ann Arbor.

Zimmerman, M. et al., eds. (1998) *Aspects of Apuleius' Golden Ass II: Cupid and Psyche*, Groningen.

Zimmerman, M. et al. (2004), *Apuleius Madaurensis Metamorphoses Books IV 28-35, V and VI 1-24. The Tale of Cupid and Psyche, Groningen*. (Groningen Commentaries on Apuleius).

I would like to thank Giacomo Savani for drawing the cover art, Maria Haley for her many good ideas, Stephen Harrison for reading and commenting on an earlier draft, and my family, especially Gurbir for printing the book and Amrita for wanting to tell the story of Cupid and Psyche to so many people.

Regine May January 2019

CHAPTER ONE

Psyche's beauty

4 *.28*
In a certain city there lived a king and a queen, who had three beautiful daughters. The older two were both very pretty, but it was still possible to compliment them with human praise. The loveliness of the youngest girl, however, was so special, so splendid, that it could not be expressed or sufficiently praised in our poor human language. In fact, many citizens and plenty of strangers were excitedly drawn together by the rumour of such an excellent spectacle. They were astonished at her inaccessible beauty, and in admiration moved their right hands to their lips, their index finger placed on their outstretched thumb, so that they could idolise and worship her as if she were the goddess Venus herself.[1] And

soon word had spread through the nearest cities and bordering regions that the goddess whom the deepest blue of the sea had born and the dew of the foaming waves had raised was now walking in the middle of gatherings of common people and bestowing the favour of her divine graciousness everywhere, or at least that recently divine dewdrops had fallen from heaven and in response not the sea but the earth had grown another Venus,[2] gifted with the flower of maidenhood.

4 .29

So day by day there was more and more gossip, so her fame increased and spread widely through the nearest islands and much of the mainland and a large number of provinces. Soon many mortals gathered together after long travels over land and journeys over the deepest seas to see this glorious wonder of the age. No one sailed to Paphos any more, to Cnidos, or even to Cythera, to see the goddess Venus.[3] Her rites were suspended, her temples damaged, her ceremonial couches were trodden upon, her ceremonies neglected; her statues were ungarlanded and her deserted altars were polluted with cold ash. It was the girl who was worshipped, and the divine power of such a great goddess was revered in a human face. On the girl's morning walk it was the name of the absent Venus that was venerated with sacrifices and feasts. And when she passed through the streets, people often prayed to her with garlands and flowers. This brazen transfer of divine honours to the cult of a mortal girl strongly incensed the passions of the true Venus. Impatiently she shook her head in fury, groaned deeply, and said to herself:

4 .30

'Now look at me, I am the ancient mother of nature,[4] I am the first origin of the elements, I am Venus, the nourisher of the whole world, look at me, who am now pushed into sharing the honour of my majesty with a mortal girl! And my name, founded in heaven, is now disrespected with earthly filth! No doubt I now will have to suffer the uncertainty of sacrifices shared with a substitute goddess, and a girl fated to die will be going around in my likeness. So there was no point in that shepherd,[5] whose sense of justice and faith great Jupiter approved of, preferring me to such mighty goddesses on account of my extraordinary beauty. But that woman, whoever she is, will not get much joy out of snatching my honours. I will soon make sure that she will be sorry for that unlawful beauty of hers!'

She hurriedly called her son, that winged and rather reckless boy, who with his wicked character, contempt for public order, and weapons of torches and arrows, runs around at night through the houses of strangers and upsets everyone's marriages, and commits such shameful acts with impunity and does nothing good at all.[6] Although he was already by his own nature undisciplined and unruly, Venus spurred him on above and beyond that.

· · ·

4 .31

She led him to that city and showed him Psyche[7] – for this was the girl's name – in person. She also told him the whole story about her rival's beauty, and said, moaning and groaning with exasperation:

'I beg you by the bonds of motherly love, by the sweet wounds of your arrows, by the honey-sweet burns of that torch of yours, avenge your mother, avenge me completely, and take severe revenge on that insolent beauty. Do this one and only thing willingly, that's all: let that girl be seized by the most violent passion for the lowest of men, a man doomed by Fortune to have neither status, wealth nor health, and so wretched that he could not find his equal on the whole wide world in his misery.'

After she said that, she kissed her son lingeringly and with gentle pressure, her lips parted, and made for the nearest coast where the tide swept over the beach, and stepped with her rosy feet on the foam on top of the swirling surf.[8] And look! The deepest sea settled in a clear eddy. And what she had barely begun to wish for happened immediately as if she had ordered it already in advance: the ocean's homage to her did not delay. There were the daughters of Nereus singing a choral song, and bristly Portunus with his deep blue beard, Salacia loaded with fish in her lap, and little Palaemon the dolphin-charioteer. Now flocks of Tritons jumped everywhere through the seas: one blew soft melodies on his conch-shell, another one battled the hostile blaze of the sun with a silken sunshade; yet another one carried a mirror before his mistress' eyes, others were yoked together and swam underneath her chariot. So great was the army accompanying Venus on her procession to the Ocean.

4 *.32*

In the meantime, despite her eye-catching beauty, Psyche gained no advantage at all for herself from her allure. She was stared at by everyone, praised by everyone, but no one, not a king, not a prince, not even a commoner, approached her as a suitor wishing for marriage. They did admire her divine good looks, but just as everyone admires a statue fashioned by an artist. Long ago already, her two older sisters, about whose more moderate beauty nobody had spread any rumours, had been engaged to royal suitors and already secured happy marriages. Psyche, however, sat at home, a maiden-widow lamenting her solitary loneliness, sick in body, wounded in mind,[9] and hating that beauty in herself which was yet most attractive to all people. So, as that most wretched father of this most unfortunate daughter suspected the hatred of the heavens and feared the anger of the powers above, he consulted the most ancient oracle of the Milesian god.[10] To this great god he prayed with prayers and sacrifices, seeking a marriage and a husband for the slighted maiden. Apollo, although he was a Greek and Ionian, for the sake of the author of this Milesian tale responded as follows with a Latin oracle:[11]

· · ·

4 *.33*

> 'On the mountain's highest crag, king,
>   place your daughter,
> Adorned with the robes of a funereal
>   wedding. [12]
> Do not hope for a son-in-law born of
>   mortal family,
> But for a cruel and wild and serpentine
>   monster,
> That flies along on wings above the
>   aether [13] and wearies everything,
> And maims everyone with his flame and
>   his steel. [14]
> Jupiter himself trembles before him, of
>   him all gods are scared,
> The rivers shudder at him, and so do the
>   shadows of Styx.' [15]

The king, once a happy man, on hearing the announcement of the holy prophecy, returned home slowly and sadly, and unpicked for his wife the instructions of the ill-starred omen. For several days they mourned, cried and lamented. But the horrible enactment of this dreadful omen was already pressing.

Soon the equipment for this most wretched girl's marriage to death was set up. Soon the light of black wedding torches grew gloomy with ashes and soot, and the sound of the wedding pipes changed into the mournful Lydian mode;[16] the happy chant of the marriage-hymn ended in grief-stricken howling. The bride-to-be wiped away her tears with her own flame-coloured wedding veil.[17] The whole city bewailed the sad fate of the afflicted household, and a cessation of public business was at once declared in agreement with communal mourning.

4

.34

But the heavenly commands had to be obeyed, and they claimed poor little Psyche for her destined punishment. Therefore, when the ceremonies for her marriage to death had been completed in deepest anguish, Psyche the living corpse was led away in tears. All the people followed her, and she accompanied not her wedding procession, but her funeral cortège. And whereas her parents, distraught and upset by such a disastrous event, hesitated to commit such a wicked crime, their daughter admonished them herself with these words:[18]

'Why do you torture your unhappy old age with constant crying? Why do you tire out your spirit, or rather my own, with repeated wailing? Why do you stain your faces that I revere with useless tears? Why do you damage my eyes by damaging yours? Why are you tearing out your white hair? Why do you beat your chests, why your sacred breasts? These will be your splendid rewards for my renowned beauty. Too late do you realise that you are stricken by the deadly blow of malevolent Envy. When people and whole nations were celebrating me with divine honours, when they declared me the new Venus with one single voice, then you should have grieved, then you should have cried, then you should have mourned me as if I were already dead. Now I feel, now I see that I have perished because of Venus' name alone. Take me and place me on the cliff to which the oracle has ordered me. I rush to enter upon this happy marriage, I rush to see that noble husband of mine. Why should I delay, why should I recoil from him who is coming to me, and who is born to bring ruin to the whole world?'

4 *.35*

After she had said this, the maiden fell silent, and joined the procession of the people who accompanied her with a steady stride. They came to the allotted cliff of the steep mountain, placed the girl on its highest summit as decreed, and then all left her there alone. They left behind there the wedding torches, with which they had lighted their way, and which had been extinguished by their tears. With their head bowed they prepared to go home. Her wretched parents, however, exhausted by this great calamity, shut themselves away in the darkness of their closed-up house, abandoning themselves to endless night.

Psyche, however, fearful, shaking and crying on the summit of the cliff, was carried away by a gentle breeze of the softly breathing Zephyr,[19] with her clothes flapping here and there and billowing into an arc behind her. He raised her slowly with his calm breath and carried her gradually along the slopes of the lofty crag, and laid her down gently in the bosom of the flowering meadow in the valley below.

CHAPTER TWO

Psyche's mysterious husband

5 .1

When Psyche pleasingly reclined in a soft and grassy place on her own bed of dewy herbs, the great turmoil in her mind calmed down, and she fell into sweet sleep. And when she was sufficiently refreshed by her slumber, she rose with her mind at ease.[1] She saw a grove planted with tall and massive trees, she saw a spring all translucent with glassy water. At the very centre of the grove, near the flowering spring, there was a royal palace, built not by human hands, but with divine skills. You would know already on first entrance that you are looking at an excellent and charming country lodge of some god.

For golden columns reached up to high coffered ceilings carefully carved from citrus-wood and ivory. All the walls were covered in embossed silver, with wild beasts and tame animals of the same material meeting the eyes of those who entered. Certainly that man who with such great artistic workmanship had given wild life to silver was an absolute wonder-worker, or rather a demigod or god for sure. Yes, even the floors themselves were divided up into various kinds of pictures in mosaics made from tiny precious stones. Truly, twice happy or even more blessed are those who tread upon gemstones and jewellery! The rest of the house, extending far and wide, which was precious beyond price, and all its walls that were built from massive gold shone with their own radiance, so that the house itself could provide its own sunlight, even if the sun were to refuse to. Thus the rooms, thus the colonnades, thus even the doors were gleaming. The rest of the riches matched in the same way that the greatness of the house, so that indeed one might think that this was a celestial palace made for great Jupiter to use for his dealings with humans.

5 .2

Psyche, enticed by the delights of such a place, stepped closer and, a little more confidently, crossed over the threshold. Soon her eagerness tempted her to examine every single thing in this most beautiful of sights, and on the other side of the building she noticed store rooms built with sublime art and stuffed full with great treasure. There was nothing that was not there. But beyond her astonishment at such great riches, it especially amazed her that this treasure trove of all the world was not safeguarded by chain, lock, or guard. As she was looking at this with greatest pleasure, some voice bereft of a body addressed itself to her:[2]

'Mistress,' it said, 'why are you so astonished by such wealth? All these things are yours. Retire from here to your bedchamber, and refresh your tiredness on your bed, and take a bath if you like. We, whose voices you hear, are your servant women and will attend to you sedulously, nor will a royal feast take long to appear once you have taken care of your body's needs.'

5 .3 Psyche felt the blessings of divine providence on herself, and listened to the advice of the disembodied voice. She washed away her tiredness first with sleep and then a bath; and immediately there appeared in front of her a raised semi-circular platform; believing because of the dinner equipment on it that it was set out for her own refreshment, she lay down to dinner cheerfully. And straightaway there were trays plentiful with nectar-sweet wine and various foods, although no one was serving them up, but they were placed before her as if pushed there by some breath of air alone. She was not able to see anyone, but only heard words uttered and had only voices as her maids. After her opulent dinner someone invisible entered and sang, and another played a lyre,

which itself was invisible, too. Then the sound of a group singing together in harmony reached her ears, so that, even though no human being was visible, still it was clear that this was a choir.

5 .4

When these pleasures had come to an end, and the evening star's arrival suggested it was late, Psyche retired to bed. It was already quite late in the night, when a gentle sound reached her ears. Then she feared for her maidenhood and felt very lonely, so she shuddered and shivered, and was even more afraid of something bad happening to her because she did not know what it might be. Soon her unknown husband arrived, climbed into her bed, made Psyche his wife, and left quickly before sunrise.[3] At once, voices like ladies-in-waiting in her bedroom took care of the new bride whose maidenhood was over. This went on for a long time. And as it is usually happens naturally, the novelty of her situation began to give pleasure to her by continuously familiarising her with it, and the sound of the intangible voice provided comfort in her loneliness.

In the meantime, her parents were growing old with tireless grief and mourning, and as the story spread more widely, her older sisters heard all about it. Hastily they left their homes in sorrow and sadness, and competed with each other in their race to see and speak to their parents.

· · ·

5

.5

On that night, her husband addressed his Psyche, for she could sense him very clearly with her hands and ears, though not with her eyes: 'My sweetest Psyche, my beloved wife, merciless Fortune is threatening you with deadly danger, and I advise you to guard against it with most pressing caution. Your sisters are now disturbed by their belief that you are dead. They are following your tracks and are about to arrive at that rock. If you happen to hear any of their lamentations, you should neither respond nor even look that way at all, or else you will cause me the deepest anguish, but for yourself utter destruction.'

She agreed and vowed to act according to her husband's judgment. But when both he and the night had slipped away, the poor girl spent the whole day in tears and laments, crying again and again that now she had truly and completely died, because she was locked up and under guard in her beautiful prison, and deprived of conversation and exchange with human beings.[4] She could not even bring help and support to her sisters who were mourning her, or even see them at all. Unrestored by r bathing, food or any kind of refreshment, she retired to sleep, crying profusely.

· · ·

5 .6

Hardly any time passed; she was still weeping when her husband got into her bed a little earlier than usual and embraced her, and complained: 'Is this what you promised me, my Psyche? What should I expect from you now, I, your husband? What should I hope for? All day and all night, even during our loving embraces you do not stop torturing yourself. Well then, do as you wish now, and obey your heart even though it asks for its own ruin. Only remember my serious warnings, when it is too late and you start feeling sorry for this.' Then with prayers and threats that she was about to die she forced her husband to agree to her desires, that she might see her sisters, soothe their grief, and speak with them face to face. So he yielded to the prayers of his new bride and moreover permitted her to give to them as presents whatever gold and jewellery she wanted to; but repeatedly he warned her and often intimidated her so as never to be persuaded by the wicked counsel of her sisters and never to enquire about the appearance of her husband, or else, because of her impious curiosity she would throw herself from the height of her fortune to rock bottom and never ever again enjoy his embrace.

She thanked her husband, already happier in her mind, and said: 'But I would rather die a hundred times than lose this sweet marriage of ours. For I love you passionately, whoever you are, and consider you as dear to me as my life's breath, and don't think even Cupid your equal.[5] But please, I beg you, grant me this request and order your servant Zephyr to set my sisters here for me by the same transport as before.' Then she gave him persuasive kisses and heaped charming words on him and wrapped around him her compelling arms, and added this to her endearments 'My honey, my husband, you sweet soul of your Psyche.' Reluctantly, her husband yielded to the strength and force of her loving whisperings and promised that he would do everything, and then, as daylight broke, he vanished from his wife's embrace.

5 .7

But those sisters, after investigating where the rock was and the place where Psyche had been left behind, quickly rushed there, and started to cry their eyes out and beat their breasts, until the rocks and cliffs were rebounding with the echoes of their constant wails. Next they called for their poor sister by her proper name, until the piercing sound of their bawling voices slipped down the drop and Psyche ran from her house frantic and trembling, and said: 'Why are you destroying yourselves pointlessly with your wretched laments? The one you are mourning, me, I'm here. Stop your grieving and at last dry your cheeks wet from ceaseless crying, because now you can embrace her whom you were lamenting.'

Then she called Zephyr and advised him of her husband's command. Immediately he obeyed the order and directly carried them down, transporting them harmlessly on the softest of breezes. Soon the sisters enjoyed their mutual embraces and hurried kisses, and the same tears that had been calmed before now came back again as their happiness urged them on.

'But come in happiness under my roof and into my house', Psyche said, 'and refresh your tormented souls together with your Psyche.'

5 .8 After addressing them like this, she displayed the large riches of the golden house and the crowded household of servant voices to their eyes and ears, and refreshed them lavishly with the most beautiful bath and the superhuman sumptuousness of her tables, so that they were overwhelmed with the copious treasures of these quite divine riches. They began to nurture envy deep in their hearts. Finally, one of them did not cease to interrogate her quite meticulously and diligently: who was the master of these heavenly things, who and what was her husband? But Psyche did not in any way violate her husband's command or drive it out from the secret places of her heart, but on the spur of the moment she made up a lie that he was a young and handsome man, just now darkening his cheeks with a downy beard, and that he was generally busy with hunting in the fields and in the mountains.[6] But for fear that she might betray her silent plan with a slip if the conversation continued, she loaded them with wrought gold and gem-encrusted necklaces,

immediately called Zephyr and handed them over to him to carry them back.

5 .9

As this was carried out immediately, those worthy sisters returned home and, already jealously aflame with growing envy, screeched loudly to each other. Finally, one of them began to speak: 'O blind and cruel and unjust Fortune! Did this truly please you, that we, born from the same two parents, should suffer such a different fate? And that we, who are older, were handed over to foreign husbands as slaves, missing both our home and our country, living in exile separated far from our parents, while this one here, the youngest, the one last birth that an already tired womb popped out, acquired such riches and a god as her husband? She doesn't even know how to use all that wealth of goods properly! Did you see, sister, how numerous and how fine the necklaces were that were lying around in that house, how the dresses gleamed and the gemstones sparkled, and how much gold was under our feet everywhere? But if she really has such a handsome husband as she claims, there is no woman luckier than her in the whole wide world. Perhaps even, when they are getting used to each other more and more, and their affection for each other gets stronger, her husband god might make her a goddess, too. That's it, by Hercules![7] That's why she was behaving and conducting herself like that. That is already where that woman is setting her sights, aspiring to her own godhead, she who has voices as maids and gives commands to the winds themselves! Poor me, on the other hand: firstly, I got allotted a husband older than my father, and secondly he is balder than a pumpkin and punier than a baby, and he locks up the whole house with bolts and chains.'[8]

5 *.10*

The other one picked this up: 'And I – I have to endure a husband bent over and crippled with arthritis, and therefore he hardly ever rekindles the fires of my passion. Constantly I have to rub his fingers because they are twisted and hardened into stone, and I am burning up these delicate hands of mine with smelly salves and dirty bandages and stinking plasters, and I don't maintain the dutiful appearance of a wife, but play the exhausting role of a nurse. It's up to you sister, to see for yourself with how much patience, or rather servility – I am going to say freely what I think – you might like to bear this. As far as I am concerned, I can't stomach any longer that such a blessed fortune has fallen into the lap of our unworthy sister. Just remember how condescending she was, how arrogantly she behaved with us. How she betrayed her puffed up mind by that very boasting with her shameless showiness, and how she unwillingly tossed to us such small amounts of such great riches, and then immediately troubled by our presence she ordered us to be thrust out, hissed off and blown away. I wouldn't be a woman, nor would I have any breath in me if I didn't cast her down to the ground from such great heights of riches. And if, as it should, this insult to us pricked you, too, let's both try to come up with a compelling plan. First, let's not show any of the things we are carrying to our parents or to anyone else, or, rather, let's pretend we know nothing about her safety. It's enough that we ourselves have seen what we are sorry to have seen; by no means should we reveal to our parents and the population as a whole such joyful news about her. Those people are not wealthy whose riches no one knows about. She will learn that she does not have maidservants, but older sisters. And now, let us retreat to our husbands and return to our poor but quite respectable houses, and when we have come up with firmer ideas, let's return strengthened in order to punish her arrogance.'

5 .11

This evil plan pleased both evil sisters well. After they had hidden all those precious gifts, they tore out their hair and scratched their cheeks, just as they deserved, and they again resumed their feigned laments. In this way they tore open again their parents' wounds of pain and scared them off straight away. Swollen with frenzy they hurried to their own houses, to construct their wicked treachery, or rather murder, against their innocent sister.

In the meantime, Psyche's husband, the one she did not know, once again warned her in his nightly tête-à-têtes with her: 'Don't you see how dangerous this is for you?

Fortune is now shooting at you from afar, and if you don't take very strong precautions in advance, she will soon battle with you hand to hand.[9] Those treacherous she-wolves are making great attempts to prepare a wicked trap for you: the gist of it is to persuade you to investigate my face, which, as I have told you many times, you will not see again once you have seen it. Therefore, if hereafter those most vile Lamiae[10] come back here, armed with their harmful thoughts – and they will come again, I know you must not speak to them at all; and if you are not able to bear this because of your simple nature and soft heart, at least don't listen to them and say absolutely nothing about your husband. For we are about to enlarge our own family, and your womb, like a child's until now, is bearing us another child, who, if you shield our secret with silence, will be a god, but if you betray it, human.'[11]

5 .12

At that news Psyche flourished with happiness, applauded the reassurance of a divine child, and delighted in the honour of the word 'mother'. She anxiously counted the increasing days and the outgoing months, and in her first lesson about the burden she knew nothing about she wondered how her fruitful womb could swell up because of such a small pinprick.

But already those pests, those most disgusting Furies were setting sail, breathing viperous venom and rushing with unsisterly speed.[12] Then for the second time her fleeting husband warned his Psyche: 'This is the final day, the last chance! Your own gender is hostile to you, your own flesh and blood is your enemy, and they have already taken up arms against you, set up camp against you, positioned a battle line against you and sounded the charge against you. Already your evil sisters have drawn the dagger and aim for your throat. Oh, my sweetest Psyche, what great calamities are pressing down on us! Have mercy on yourself and me, and save with pious self-control your house, your husband, yourself and our little one from the imminent ruinous misfortune that threatens us. Those wicked women – you cannot call them your sisters, with their murderous hatred as they trample the bonds of blood with their feet – do not look at them or hear them out, when they stretch out from the cliff just like Sirens and cause the rocks to resound with their deadly voices.'[13]

5 .13 Hesitatingly, Psyche replied with tearful sighs: 'For a long time already, as far as I know, you have assessed the proofs of my loyalty and my discretion, and now you will also be able to confirm my strength of mind in the same way. You just once again give orders to our friend Zephyr, let him do his job, and instead of your own most holy appearance which is denied to me, at least give me a glance at my sisters. By your cinnamon-scented locks hanging round your face, by your tender and smooth cheeks that are so similar to mine, by your breast warm with an unknown passion, as I hope to discover your face at least in our little one: be prevailed upon by the faithful

prayers of a restless suppliant, and grant me the delight of embracing my sisters, and refresh the soul of your Psyche, who is devoted and dedicated to you, with joy. I shall seek no further information about your face. Not even the darkness of the night will hold me back, because I hold you in my arms, light of my life.'

Enchanted by these words and her soft embraces, her husband dried her tears with his curls and promised he would do what she wanted, and immediately left to move before the light of the young day came.

5 .14

The sister team, bonded together by their schemes, did not even visit their parents, and travelled straight from their ships to the cliff with headlong speed; they did not even wait for the presence of the wind to carry them, but jumped into the abyss with unrestrained recklessness. But Zephyr, remembering the royal edict, caught them, though reluctantly, in the lap of his breathing breeze, and set them down on the ground. Immediately these women joined in lock step without hesitation and gained entrance to the house. They embraced their prey, deceitful and sisters in name only, and covering the treasure-vault of their deeply hidden treachery with happy faces, they flattered Psyche like this: 'Psyche, you are not so little any more as you used to be, and now you yourself are a mother! Just think how many good things for us you are carrying in that little pouch of yours! You will bring so much happiness and delight to our whole house! We are so lucky and will have so much fun bringing up this golden child! If he bears any resemblance to the beauty of his parents, as he should, he will be born a true Cupid.'[14]

5 .15

And so with fake affection they slowly invaded the mind of their sister. As soon as they were refreshed from their travel-fatigue by sitting down, and restored with the steamy waters of the baths, Psyche entertained them most beautifully in her dining room with quite wonderful and abundant delicacies and titbits. She commanded a cithara to play – there was lyre-plucking; some pipes to perform – there was fluting; some choirs to sing – there was chanting. Even though no one was to be seen, all these things soothed their audience's spirits with the sweetest melodies. But not even the honeyed sweetness of this song could restrain the villainy of these vile women; instead, they moved the conversation to the cunning trap they had planned, put on their act and began to enquire what sort of man her husband was, where he was from, and what kind of occupation he had. Then Psyche in her excessive simplicity forgot her previous story and invented a new explanation. She said that her husband was from a near-by province, that he was a trader dealing with a lot of money, and already middle-aged, with a little grey already peppered throughout his hair. But she did not continue that conversation with them even a little bit longer, and loaded them once again with sumptuous presents and handed them over to their windy carriage.

5 .16

But while they were returning home, lifted up high by Zephyr's peaceful breath, they argued among themselves: 'What, sister, can we say about that foolish girl's monstrous lie? At first he was a young man, hardly yet growing a beard of fine down, and now he is middle-aged with shiny bright white hair? Who could that be whom a short space of time has transformed with such sudden onset of old age? You'll find that there is no other solution, my sister: either this horrible girl has fabricated a lie, or she does not know what her husband looks like. Whichever of these possibilities is correct, she has to be ousted from these riches as soon as possible. If she doesn't know the face of her husband, she is clearly married to a god, and bears us a god in that pregnancy of hers. For sure, if she – heaven forbid – were to be known as the mother of a divine child, I will hang myself at once.[15] Therefore, in the meantime let's return to our parents and let's weave some tricks of the same colour to add to the frame of this conversation.'

5 .17

All fired up like that, they greeted their parents haughtily and stayed awake through a restless night. Early in the morning, these accursed women flew up to the cliff, and from there with the wind's usual protection flew down; they forced out tears by pressing on their eyelids and greeted the girl with this cunning deceit: 'Here you are, sitting cheerfully and happy in your ignorance of such a great harm, and indifferent to the danger to yourself. We, on the other hand, were lying awake all night because we were worried about your situation and were miserably tortured by your misfortunes. Because now we know the truth, we cannot hide it from you, for we are allies in your pain and fate: a massive snake, creeping along with many-knotted twists, its neck bloody with harmful venom and its deep craw gaping wide open, lies with you at night in secret.[16] Remember now the Pythian oracle,[17] which declared that you were destined for marriage with a savage beast! Many smallholders, men who hunt around here, and quite a few farmers have seen him returning in the evening from his feeding and swimming in the shallows of the nearby river.

5.*18*

They all confirm that it will not fatten you up with respect and pleasant food for much longer now; instead, as soon as your full womb has completed your pregnancy and you are given your labour's most precious fruit, it will devour you! It is now your choice how to react to this: either you might want to agree with your sisters who are concerned for your precious safety, avoid death, and live safe from danger and with us, or you might be buried in the guts of this most savage of beasts. But if this

27

countryside loneliness with its voices, or the stinking and dangerous embraces with your furtive lover, or the hugs with a poisonous snake make you happy, at least we your caring sisters have done our duty.'

Then poor little Psyche, simple and soft-hearted as she was, was gripped with great horror at their grim words. Driven out of her own mind, she completely dropped all memory of her husband's many warnings and her promises, and threw herself head first into the depths of disaster. Shaking, pale from her blood deserting her face, just able to stammer some words in whispers with half-open lips, she slurred her reply to them:

5 *.19*

'You, my dearest sisters, as is only right, keep to the obligations of your family duty. And, for a fact, these people who confirmed these things to you don't seem to be making up lies, either. I have never seen my husband's face, and I have no idea where he is from; I hear his voice only a little at night, and endure a husband of uncertain status who is a complete refugee from daylight; I absolutely agree with you when you quite rightly say that he is some beast. He always scares me away vigorously from looking at his face, and threatens me with great reprisals if I were to show any curiosity about his appearance. Now, if you are able to offer any help and assistance to your sister in danger, help me now. Or else any neglect from now on would destroy all your previous providence and good deeds.'

The gates were thrown wide open now, and these criminal women had got hold of their sister's unprotected heart; they dropped their concealments and uncovered their artillery, and with their swords of deception unsheathed they invaded the fearful thoughts of that simple girl.

5

.20

Finally, one of them said: 'Since our family connection forces us to scorn all danger where your safety is concerned, we will show you the only available path to your salvation, a way we have been thinking about for a very long time. Take a very sharp razor, sharpened even more by applying your little palm to smooth it, and hide it secretly on the side of the bed where you tend to sleep. Then make ready a lamp, full of oil and shining with clear light, and hide it under the cover of some little vessel. Be sure to conceal all these preparations. After he has slithered inside with his furrowed trails and climbed into the bed as usual, and when he is already stretched out and rolled up overpowered by his first heavy slumber, and has started to breathe deeply, then you slip down off your bed and make small steps with bare feet and on tiptoe; free the oil lamp from the prison of its blinding darkness, take the light's suggestions for the best chance for your magnificent deed; be fearless and grasp your double-edged weapon, first lift up your right hand, then with the strongest effort you can possibly muster, cut off the head of that poisonous snake from where it is joined to its neck. Nor will you miss out on our help; as soon as you have gained your safety with his death, we will wait anxiously to fly to you, and we will carry all these things here away together with you as swiftly as possible, and then arrange for a desirable marriage for you, human to human.'

5 *.21*

Because Psyche was already on fire, they set their sister's smouldering heart ablaze with such a kindling of words. They immediately left her, because they were extremely afraid to be themselves found in the vicinity of such a great crime. They were carried over the cliff by the usual blowing of the winged wind, and there and then they rushed away head over heels in flight, immediately boarded their ships, and went away.

But Psyche, left alone, even though she was not alone as she was pursued by aggressive Furies[18], was floating in her anguish like on the waves of the sea. Although she had already made up both her plan and her mind, when she applied her hand to the crime, she wavered, uncertain of her decision, torn apart by the many passions caused by her dilemma. She dashed and delayed; she dared and she trembled; she despaired and she flew into a rage; and, worst of all, in the same body she hated the beast but loved the husband. But when evening dragged on into night, she hurried to set up the equipment for her horrendous crime in haste. Night came, and her husband came, and after a skirmish on love's battlefield he fell into a deep sleep.

. . .

5 *.22*

Then Psyche, though otherwise weak in body and mind, was made stronger by the help of cruel Fate's ferocity. She brought out the oil lamp and grasped the razor, and in her courage changed her sex. But as soon as the light was brought forward, and the secrets of her bed became clear, she saw of all wild creatures the tamest and sweetest beast, Cupid himself, the beautiful god sleeping beautifully. At this sight even the light of the oil lamp flashed up cheerfully, and the razor began to regret its blasphemous sharpness. Psyche, too, was shocked at this magnificent sight and quite lost her mind; fainting with pale exhaustion, she trembled and sank down to her knees; she sought to plunge the blade, but in her own heart. She would certainly have succeeded with this, if the blade had not jumped out of her careless hands in horror at such a crime and flown away. Psyche was now already tired and with weakened health, but when she looked over and over again at the beauty of that divine face, her mind began to revive.

She saw the lively hair tumbling from his golden head drenched with ambrosia,[19] ringlets gracefully arranged rambling over his milk white neck and his rosy cheeks, some hanging down the front, others over his back; at their extraordinary gleaming splendour the light of the oil lamp itself began to flicker. Across the shoulders of the winged god dewy feathers were shining with glittering brightness, and although his wings were at repose, tiny little plumes at their very edges, most tender and delicate, were quivering and bouncing mischievously and restlessly. The rest of his body was smooth and splendid, so that even Venus could not be ashamed of having given birth to him. At the foot of the dainty bed there were lying a bow, a quiver and arrows, the auspicious weapons of the mighty god.

5 .23

When Psyche, with an eager and rather curious mind, explored and stroked and admired her husband's weapons, she took out one single arrow from the quiver. She was about to test its sharp point with the tip of her thumb, but pricked it a little too deep with rather too strong an effort of her trembling fingers, so that tiny little drops of rose-red blood were trickling over the surface of her skin. So, unknowingly, by her own doing, Psyche fell in love with Love. Then, more and more burning with desire for the god of Desire, she bent over him, desperately catching her breath, and as she quickly heaped kisses upon him with parted and passionate lips, she began to fear his sleep might not be deep enough. But while she was wavering, her wounded heart excited by so great a blessing, that very oil lamp, either through the worst kind of treachery or through harmful jealousy, or because it longed itself to touch such a body and practically kiss it, sputtered from the top of its flame a drop of boiling oil on to the right shoulder of the god.

Oh, you rash and reckless lamp, you worthless servant of

Love, you burn the very god of all fire, when of course it was some lover who invented you in the first place so that he might enjoy longer possession at night of what he desired!

Burnt like that, the god jumped up, and once he felt tainted by his trust being betrayed, he immediately flew away from the kisses and embraces of his most unhappy wife, and that in complete silence.

5

.24

But Psyche quickly grasped with both hands his right leg, while he was rising, a miserable passenger to his soaring transportation, and a lowly follower of dangling company through the cloudy expanses of the sky; at last, tired out she fell to the ground.[20] Her divine lover did not desert her when she was lying on the earth, but flew to the nearest cypress tree, and from its highest top he addressed her, deeply distressed.

'My naïve little Psyche, I disregarded the orders of my mother Venus, who had commanded me to tie you in desire to a poor man of very low status, and condemn you to the lowest kind of marriage. Instead I myself flew to you as your lover. But this I did, carelessly, I know, and I, that famous archer, struck myself with my very own weapon and made you my wife, only for me to seem a beast to you and for you to try to cut my head off with a dagger – that head which bears these eyes that are in love with you. Again and again I kept advising you that you should be careful about this. I kept warning you against this gently. But those celebrated counsellors of yours will pay the price to me straightaway for their destructive advice: you, on the other hand, I shall only punish by my departure.'

And as soon as his speech came to an end he rushed off into the skies on his wings.

5 .25

Psyche, however, lay prostrate on the ground, and watched her husband flying away as long as her eyesight let her, and tortured her soul with unrestrained wailing. But as soon as the great distance had taken her husband far away from her, as he was carried away on the twin oarage of his wings, she threw herself head first from the bank of the nearest river.[21] But the gentle stream, in honour of the god, for sure, who was in the habit of setting even water on fire, fearful for himself, immediately carried her on his harmless waves and set her down on his shore flowering with vegetation.

Then Pan, that rustic god, happened to be sitting near the edge of the river, embracing Echo the mountain goddess and teaching her to repeat tunes of all sorts to him.[22]

Close to the shore, wandering and grazing, his she-goats were cropping the river's greenery. The goat-god gently called the love-sick and exhausted Psyche over to him, as he was somehow not unaware of her fate, and comforted her with calming words:

'Pretty girl, I'm only a rustic fellow and a goatherd, but I have the benefit of advanced old age and much experience. Now, if I guess correctly – that is surely what wise men call divination – from your wavering and quite often staggering gait, from that extreme pallor of your body and your constant sighs, and even more so from your grieving eyes, you are suffering from desperate love. Therefore listen to me, and don't try to make away with yourself again, whether by jumping from a great height nor by any other kind of death you might opt for. Stop mourning and put aside your grief, and rather worship Cupid the greatest of gods with your prayers, and seek to earn the favour of that utterly pampered and spoilt young man with charming compliance.'

5 *.26*

When the shepherd god had stopped talking, Psyche made no reply, but merely a gesture of respect to that helpful divine being, and kept going. But after she had wandered with laborious steps along a rather long way, when the day was already coming to an end, on some unknown path she approached a certain city, in which the husband of one of her sisters held power. When Psyche realised this, she requested her presence to be announced to her sister. Soon she was shown in, and they took their fill of mutual embraces and greetings of each other. When her sister asked after the reasons for her arrival, Psyche began to speak:

'You remember your counsel of course, when you both advised me that I should destroy the beast that was lying with me under the assumed name of "husband" with a two-edged razor, before it could gobble poor me up with its greedy maw. I agreed. But as soon as I set eyes on his face (the lamp was my accomplice), I saw a wonderful and completely divine spectacle, the son of the goddess Venus himself – Cupid himself, I tell you – asleep in gentle slumber. But when I got excited by such a blessed spectacle, and confused by the excessive amount of pleasure, I suffered from my inability to enjoy it, and of course by the worst kind of accident the lamp bubbled forth a drop of burning oil onto his shoulder. That pain immediately jolted him out of his sleep, and when he spotted me armed with iron and fire, he said: "You! Because of this cursed crime, at once divorce yourself from my marriage bed, and take with you your property. As far as I am concerned, I will now make your sister – and here he spoke the name by which you are known – my wife in a most sacred wedding ceremony."[23] And at once he ordered Zephyr to blow me away beyond the boundaries of his house.'

5 .27

Before Psyche had even finished her speech, her sister, driven by the stings of crazy lust and harmful envy, on the spot concocted a lie and deceived her husband, claiming that she had heard some news about the death of her parents. She immediately boarded a boat and made at once for that cliff. A different wind was blowing, but she panted in blind hope, and cried: 'Welcome me, Cupid, a wife worthy of you, and you, Zephyr, lift up your mistress!'

And with a great leap she threw herself down the cliff. Yet not even in death could she reach that place she wished for, as her limbs were tossed and torn apart over craggy rocks and, just as she deserved, her body was ripped apart, and she died, offering a ready meal for the birds and beasts.[24]

The second act of revenge and retribution was not delayed, either. For Psyche, again with wandering steps, reached another city, where her other sister was dwelling in a similar style. She was seduced by the same sisterly deception in exactly the same way. Eager to replace her sister in an immoral marriage, she hurried to the cliff and fell to a similar death.

5 *.28*

In the meantime, Psyche was intent on searching for Cupid, and went around many peoples; but he, in pain from the lamp wound, lay sighing in his mother's own bedroom. Then a very white bird, the seagull who skirts on its wings across the floods of the sea, dived quickly into the deepest bosom of the ocean.[25] There it perched next to Venus who was bathing and swimming there, and told her that her son had been burnt, that he was grieving in deep pain from this wound, and that his recovery was in doubt. Also, that the whole household of Venus was being maligned by word of mouth of all peoples with rumours and all kinds of gossip, that 'You two have both retreated: he to dallying with women in the mountains, and you to swimming in the seas. And because of this, there is no pleasure any more, no grace, no charm. Instead, everything is unkempt, rustic, and horrible. There are no longer any weddings, no friendships, no alliances, there is no longer any love for children, but instead there is the enormous squalor and unpleasant disgust of sleazy couplings.'

These were the things that this chatty and rather meddlesome bird was tweeting into Venus' ears, shredding her son's reputation.

But Venus was thoroughly furious and suddenly screamed: 'Well then, that great son of mine has a girlfriend now? All right then, you who are my only devoted servant, give me the name of that girl who enticed my noble and innocent boy! Is she one of the tribe of the Nymphs, or one of the number of the Hours, or one of the choir of Muses, or one of my attendants, the Graces?'[26]

That garrulous bird did not shut up, and said: 'I don't know, mistress. But if I remember correctly, they say that he is desperately in love with a girl called Psyche.'

Then Venus screamed out loud with rage: 'Psyche? It is really true that he loves that rival of my beauty, that usurper of my name? No doubt that brat of mine mistook me for a seedy matchmaker who pointed a girl out to him so that he should get to know her!'

• • •

5 *.29*

Protesting in this way she emerged quickly from the sea and immediately made for her own golden bedroom, where she found her poorly boy, just as she had heard she would. Just from inside the doorway she already roared as loudly as she could: 'Fine carryings-on these, worthy of your birth and your character! First you trample with your feet your mother's orders – or should I say your ruler's – by not torturing my enemy with base love affairs! And next, you, a boy of this tender age, hold her in your wanton and immature embraces, thinking of course that I would accept an enemy as my daughter-in-law! But when you imagine even for a moment, you joker, you unlovable seducer, that you are the only one fit to have babies, and I am no longer able to have children because of my age, I want you to know that I will give birth to another son much, much better than you. Or rather, so that you feel the insult even more, I am going to adopt one of my young house slaves and will gift him those wings of yours and the torches and the bow and even the arrows and all the rest of my equipment, which I didn't give you to put to that kind of use! For there was no allowance at all from your father's estate for that kind of kit.[27]

• • •

5

.30

But you were brought up badly from earliest childhood; you have quick hands and so many times you have punched your elders disrespectfully. Even me, your very own mother, you expose on a daily basis, you parent killer, and you have pricked me quite often and despise me as if I were a helpless widow! You don't even have any respect for your stepfather, that bravest of men and greatest of warriors![28] And why should you? Quite often have you presented him with girlfriends and caused me distress at his adultery! But now I will make sure that you are sorry for this little game, and your marriage will have a sour and bitter taste! But I, what should I do, now that I am a laughing stock? Where should I turn? How could I restrain this reptile? Should I seek help from my enemy Sobriety, whom I have offended so many times because of this fellow's wantonness?[29] No, I shudder at the mere thought of having to talk to that boorish and squalid woman! Still, the consolation of revenge by hook or by crook shouldn't be despised. I have to employ her straightaway, and no one else. She will chastise that joker, she will take apart his quiver and disarm his arrows, unstring his bow, put out his torches, yes, she will restrain his body itself with harsher remedies. I shall believe his insolence against me only atoned for when she has shaved off his curls, which my very own hands have stroked over and over into a golden sheen, and clipped off his wings, which I have infused with nectar in my own lap.'[30]

· · ·

5

.31

This she announced, and rushed outside, belligerently and fuming furiously, as befitted Venus. But that moment Ceres and Juno joined her, and when they saw her face swollen with anger, they asked her why she would constrain the loveliness of her brilliant eyes with such a sullen frown.[31] But she said: 'Good timing! You have come just right to accomplish the desire in my burning heart! Please, with all your powers, search out Psyche, my elusive fugitive, for me! For sure this notorious story about my household and the deeds of my unspeakable son can't have passed you by.'

Then those two, fully aware of what had happened, undertook to appease Venus' wild wrath: 'Oh mistress, what great offence has your son committed, that you should so obstinately challenge his pleasures, and are even keen to destroy the girl he likes? What now, we ask you, is his crime, if he readily smiles at a charming girl? Or haven't you noticed that he is male and a young man, or have you really forgotten how old he is? Or, because he bears his age quite prettily, will he always seem a child to you? You are a mother, though, and what is more, a sensible woman; so will you always meddle and pry into your son's amusements, and hold him responsible for his indulgences and restrict his love affairs, and criticise your own wiles and your own delights when enacted by your handsome son? Who then among the gods, who among men, will allow you to spread desires everywhere among the people, when you yourself bitterly suppress any love affairs in your own house and close down the public workshop for women's misdeeds?'

So out of fear of his arrows, these two flattered Cupid with an obsequious defence, even though he was not there. But Venus, indignant that the insults against her were being treated with ridicule, passed past them with quick steps in the other direction and set out towards the sea.

CHAPTER THREE

Servant of Venus

6 .1
In the meantime, Psyche was driven in different directions, here and there, day and night, focused on searching for her husband. The more restless she was in mind, the more eager she was to soothe his anger, if not with a wife's endearments, then certainly, with a slave's entreaties. And when she spotted a temple on the summit of a steep mountain, she said:

'How would I know if my lord lives there?' And she quickly made her way there; although her walking was thoroughly weary from her constant toils, her hope and her desires urged her on. Soon she had diligently climbed up the rather high ridges, and she approached the shrine.

She saw ears of corn in a heap and others wound into

garlands, and ears of barley. There were sickles and all kinds of harvesting tools, but everything was lying flung everywhere and carelessly scattered and dropped down, as it happens in summer, by the hands of workmen.[1] All these things Psyche sorted diligently, arranged separately, and organised properly, in the belief of course that she should not neglect the sanctuaries and rituals of any deity, but gather the goodwill and mercy of all of them.

6.2

While she was taking care of this assiduously and conscientiously, bountiful Ceres caught sight of her, and immediately called out from afar:

'What now, poor Psyche? All over the world Venus is making anxious enquiries, tracking down your steps with fury in her heart. She is seeking you out for extreme punishment and demanding vengeance with all her divine powers. But you are here now, taking care of my things and thinking of everything else but your own safety?'

Then Psyche threw herself at the goddess' feet, drenched them in floods of tears, and swept the ground with her hair, asking her forgiveness and uttering many prayers:

'I beseech you by your fruit-giving right hand, by the joy-granting harvest rites, by the silent mysteries of your caskets, by the winged chariots of your serpent servants, by the furrows of the Sicilian fields, by the abductor's carriage and the earth that holds, by Proserpina's descent to her lightless wedding and your daughter's ascent after her light-filled discovery, and by everything else that the sanctuary in Attic Eleusis conceals in silence:[2] come to the aid of the miserable soul of Psyche, your suppliant. Let me hide only for a few short days among those heaps of corn, until the furious anger of that great goddess is mollified by the passing of time, or at least until my strength, drained by my long sufferings, is restored by a period of rest.'

6 .3

Ceres replied: 'I am truly moved by your tearful prayers and I wish to help you, but I just cannot fall out with my relative, a thoroughly good woman, with whom I also cherish a long bond of friendship. So move away from this temple at once, and think yourself lucky that you weren't detained and imprisoned by me.'

Driven out against all her hopes, Psyche, affected by doubled grief, retracted her steps. Then in a closed-in valley below she spotted, in a dimly lit grove, a temple, carefully and artfully constructed. As she did not wish to neglect any path, however doubtful, to a better hope, and wanted to curry the favour of any available deity, she stepped close to the sacred doors. She saw exquisite offerings and cloths lettered with gold attached to tree-branches and door-posts, which attested the name of the goddess to whom they were dedicated, together with expressions of gratitude for her deeds. Then Psyche knelt and embraced with both hands the altar which was still warm, wiped away her tears and prayed like this:

· · ·

6 .4

'Oh sister and wife of great Jupiter, whether you dwell in the age-old shrines of Samos, which alone glories in hosting your birth, your baby cries and your early childhood; or whether you frequent your blessed seat in lofty Carthage, which worships you as a virgin riding in the heavens on a lion; or whether near the banks of the River Inachos you preside over the ever famous walls of Argos, which now remembers you as the bride of the Thunderer and the queen of the gods; you, whom all the East venerates as Zygia the joining goddess, and all the West names as Lucina the goddess of childbirth: in my direst of sufferings, be Juno Sospita who offers help, and free me from the terror of imminent danger, me, who I am worn down by such great sufferings. As far as I know, you freely tend to come to the aid of pregnant women in peril.'[3]

Suddenly Juno manifested herself to the girl who was praying to her in this way, with all the majestic authority of her godhead, and replied right away: 'How I wish, in faith, I could match my divine will to your prayers. But decency does not allow me to go against the wishes of Venus, my daughter-in-law, whom I have always loved as if she were my daughter. Then, too, I am prevented by laws which forbid anyone from sheltering other people's runaway slaves against their masters' wishes.'

· · ·

6 .5
Psyche was utterly alarmed by this second shipwreck of her fortunes, and now unable to reach her winged husband. So she abandoned all hope for her salvation and debated with herself in this way: 'Now then, what other relief can be tried or given to my sufferings, since not even the commendations of goddesses, even though they were willing, were able to help me? Where again, therefore, shall I turn, caught up in such great snares, under which roofs or even in which darkness could I hide, and escape the inescapable eyes of mighty Venus? Well then, why don't you channel the spirit of a man and bravely renounce your empty rays of hope? And why not hand yourself over voluntarily to your mistress and, even though it's a last-ditch attempt, mitigate her raging attacks by submission? Who knows, perhaps you might even find the one you have been searching for so long in his mother's house?'

So she prepared herself for surrender with an uncertain outcome, or rather for certain death, and deliberated with herself how she should start her upcoming entreaties.

6 .6
But Venus had given up all earthly measures for her search and set off to heaven. She ordered her chariot to be prepared, the one that Vulcan the goldsmith had carefully perfected for her with refined workmanship

and presented her with as a wedding gift at the start of their marriage. It was attractive for what the file had pared away and valuable from the loss of the gold itself. From the many birds which were housed around the chamber of their mistress, four white doves, advancing joyfully, bent their colourful necks and took up the bejewelled yoke. They picked up their mistress and flew away happily.[4] Sparrows were following the goddess' chariot, frolicking with boisterous chirping, and other birds singing sweetly with honeyed melodies announced the arrival of the goddess with sweet harmonies. The clouds made way, Heaven opened wide for his daughter,[5] and the highest aether received the goddess with joy, and great Venus' tuneful household did not have to fear aggressive eagles or rapacious hawks.

6 .7

Then she directed her steps straightaway to Jupiter's royal stronghold, and announced haughtily that she required to borrow the services of Mercury, the herald god. Jupiter nodded consent with his dark eyebrows. Triumphantly, Venus at once descended from heaven, with Mercury accompanying her, and said to him these solemn words:

'Arcadian brother,[6] you know surely that your sister Venus has never done anything without Mercury's presence, and it won't have escaped your notice for how long I haven't been able to find my runaway slave girl. Nothing else can be done now apart from your publicly announcing a reward for her discovery as my herald. Make sure, therefore, to fulfil my commission post-haste, and to describe the signs by which she can be recognised quite clearly, so that no one who might be charged with the crime of illegally concealing her could defend himself by pleading ignorance.'

With these words she handed him a pamphlet which contained Psyche's name and everything else. When she had done that, she immediately departed for home.

6 .8

Nor did Mercury fail to obey her, but he ran to and fro among all peoples, and performed his task to announce what had been entrusted to him:

'If anyone might be able to recapture her from her flight or reveal the hiding place of a runaway king's daughter, Venus' maid, by name of Psyche, he should meet up with me, Mercury the herald, behind the Murcian turning points,[7] in order to receive for his information from Venus herself seven sweet kisses and one more, sweetened like honey by the touch of her caressing tongue.'

At this announcement of Mercury's, the desire for such a great reward raised enthusiastic competition among all mortal men. These were the main reasons why now Psyche put an end to all hesitation. And when she was already getting close to her mistress' door, a member of Venus' household, by the name of Familiarisation, ran towards her, and at once exclaimed as loudly as she could:[8]

'You worthless slave, have you now finally started to realise that you have a mistress? Or will you continue to pretend with your usual insolence that you know nothing about how many trials and tribulations we have had to suffer while we were searching for you? But it's a good job that you have rather fallen into my hands, and are now caught in the very claws of Orcus;[9] and of course you can be sure that you will promptly pay the prize for your blatant disobedience!'

6.9 After she had spoken, she boldly grabbed Psyche's hair with her hands and dragged her in, even though she offered no resistance. But as soon as Venus saw her brought in and presented to her, she burst into broad guffawing laughter, as those who are furiously angry tend to do. She shook her head and scratched at her right ear, and said:

'So, you have finally chosen to pay your respects to your mother-in-law? Or have you rather come here to visit your husband, who is at great risk from the wound you gave him? But rest assured, I am going to receive you now as it is suitable for a good daughter-in-law.'

And then she called out: 'Where are Worry and Sadness, my handmaidens?'[10]

After these two had been called in, Psyche was handed over to them to be tortured. They followed their mistress' orders, and after whipping poor little Psyche and tormenting her with all other kinds of torturing equipment, they returned her to the presence of their mistress.[11] Venus yet again broke into laughter, and said:

'Oh, look, how she tries to move us to feel sorry for her with the charms of her swollen belly! No doubt she intends to make me a happy grandmother with that glorious offspring! Lucky me! Me, who in the flower of my youth will be called a grandmother, and the son of a vile slave girl will be known as the grandson of Venus! But how silly of me to speak in vain of a "son"! The marriage was between non-equals; besides, as it took place in a country house, without witnesses and without the consent of the father, it cannot be considered legitimate, and because of that this child will be born illegitimate – if indeed we will even allow you to bear it to term at all.'[12]

6.10

When she had finished, Venus flew at Psyche and ripped her dress in many places, tore her hair, boxed her head and beat her up badly. Then she picked up some wheat and barley and millet and poppy seed and chickpeas and lentils and beans, mixed them up in heaps and poured them together into a single pile, and said to her:

'As you are such an ugly slave, you seem to me to be unable to entice your lovers by any other means than with painstaking service. So I will now test your merit myself:

separate out this random pile of seeds, with every single grain allocated and sorted correctly, and show me the work is completed before this evening for my approval.'[13]

After assigning such a large pile of seeds like that, she herself departed for a wedding feast. But Psyche did not lay hands on that disorderly and unmanageable mass, and instead stood silent and stunned, confounded by this enormous order. Then a little ant – that tiny country-dwelling one – mindful of the great difficulty and work involved, in compassion for the bride of the great god and in contempt for her mother-in-law's cruelty, zealously ran here and there and called and gathered together a whole force of neighbouring ants:

'Have pity, you lively nurslings of all-mother Earth,[14] have pity, and come promptly and speedily to the aid of Cupid's wife, a pretty girl in distress!'

Waves after waves of the six-footed tribes came running, and each individual with the greatest zeal sorted out the whole pile grain by grain; and after they had divided, separated and ordered the kinds of seed, they swiftly vanished out of sight.

6 .11

At nightfall, then, Venus returned from the wedding feast, dripping with wine and smelling of balsam, her whole body garlanded with shining roses. When she saw how meticulously the miraculous labour had been completed, she said:

'This is not your work, you shameless wretch! This is not the work of your hands, but of him, who has fallen in love with you to your – or rather his own – peril!'

She threw a chunk of plain bread down for Psyche and went off to bed.

In the meantime, Cupid was being kept locked up under close guard alone in the inner parts of the house in one single room, partly so that he should not make his wound worse through impudent and wilful behaviour, and partly to keep him from meeting up with his beloved. And therefore the lovers, kept apart and separated under a single roof, spent a disagreeable and exhausting night.

But as soon as Dawn rode in, Venus summoned Psyche and addressed her with these words:

'Do you see this grove, which is spread out on the long-stretched banks of the river that washes past it, and the impassable shrubs which look down on a nearby spring? Sheep brilliant with a real fleece of pure gold wander and graze there unguarded. At once bring me from there a tuft from that fleece of precious wool, whichever way you can get it. These are my instructions.'[15]

6 *.12*

Psyche set out willingly, though not in order to complete the task, but to find a break from these problems by throwing herself off a rock into the river. But there, from out of the river, a tiny fosterer of pleasing music, divinely inspired by the soft sound of a sweet breeze, a green reed, prophesied the following:[16]

'Oh Psyche, tested by so many hardships, please do not pollute my holy waters with your most miserable death. This is also not the time to approach these fearsome sheep, as long as they borrow the intense heat of the burning sun and tend to be driven wild by violent madness; with their sharp horns and their rock-hard foreheads, and sometimes with their poisonous bites, they rage and massacre humans. But until midday has eased the sun's heat and the herd has settled down in the peacefulness of the river breeze, you will be able to escape notice by hiding under that very tall plane tree, which drinks from the same river as myself. And as soon as their madness has been softened and they have relaxed their minds, shake down the branches of the nearby grove and you will find the woolly gold that will stick everywhere on their linked trunks.'

6 *.13*

Thus a simple and humane reed showed much-suffering Psyche the way to her salvation. Nor did she regret listening carefully, once she was so carefully instructed, or cease to act, but she observed every piece of advice, and with effortless thieving she brought back a mass of soft yellow gold gathered in her lap for Venus. With her mistress, however, the danger of her second labour did not earn her a favourable reference; instead, Venus frowned and smiled bitterly, and said:

'It hasn't escaped my notice which bastard is the instigator of this deed, too. But now I will pay attention and put you to the test to see if you are genuinely equipped with a strong mind and unique intelligence. Do you see the steep mountain top looming over that sheer cliff? From this top, dark waves flow down from a black fountain and are enclosed in a basin in the nearest valley, and water the swamps of Styx and feed the harsh-sounding streams of Cocytus.[17] From just there, from the innermost bubbling of the fountainhead, draw for me some ice-cold water and bring it to me instantly in this little jar.'

With this she handed over to her a small vessel cut from crystal, and in addition to that made some even graver threats.

6.14

Psyche, though, eagerly hastened her steps and made for the highest mountain summit, undoubtedly in order to find there an end to her most wretched life. But as soon as she got to the area bordering on the above-mentioned ridge, she recognised the deadly difficulty of her enormous mission. For a tall rock of immense size, slippery and inaccessible in its ruggedness, spewed forth from stone jaws in its midst some horrible streams. These first spurted from the gaps of a sloping cleft, then flooded downhill, and, covered by the path of a sunken and narrow channel they had dug out for themselves, they plummeted unseen into the nearest valley. To its right and left – look! – there crawled out of hollowed crags fierce snakes, stretching out their long necks, their eyes given over to everlasting watchfulness and their pupils ever awake for watching and guarding. And now even the water itself defended itself, because it could speak. Over and over it screamed:

'Go away!', and 'What are you on about? Watch out!', 'What are you doing? Be careful!', and 'Run away!', and 'You will die!'. And so Psyche, by the very impossibility of her task, was turned into stone; although present in body, she was absent in mind, and completely overpowered by the weight of the dangers she could not wriggle out of, she even missed out on the ultimate consolation of tears.

6 .15

But the serious eyes of kind Providence did not overlook the sufferings of an innocent soul. For that royal bird of Jupiter the Almighty, the rapacious eagle, suddenly appeared with both wings unfolded, and in memory of that ancient service, when under the guidance of Cupid he had kidnapped the Phrygian cupbearer for Jupiter, he brought help just in time.[18] He treated with respect the god's power during his wife's toils, left behind Jupiter's ways in the highest spheres, and swooped down before the girl's eyes, and said:

'You, naïve and completely inexperienced in such things, do your really hope to be able to steal even a single drop from that most holy but no less hostile spring, or to even merely touch it? Even the gods and even Jupiter himself fear these Stygian waters, you must have heard this mentioned! And as you swear by the powers of the gods, the gods tend to swear by the majesty of Styx! Just give me that jug!'

And at once he snatched it and hurried off to fill it with water. Poised on his massive swaying wings, he directed his pair to the left and right, between the jaws of furious teeth and the quivering three-forked tongs of the dragons. Although the waters refused and warned him to fly away while he was still unharmed, he took some; he lied that he was fetching it on the order of Venus and acting as her servant, and because of this it was a little easier for him to access it.

6 .16

And so Psyche happily accepted the full jar and brought it back to Venus in haste. But even then, she still could not satisfy the will of that ferocious goddess. For threatening her with greater and crueller perils, Venus addressed her with a deadly smile:

'Well, you seem to be some extraordinarily mighty witch, I think, since you carried out my difficult orders so diligently! But you will still have to do this one job for me, darling. Take this box and direct your steps straightaway out of the daylight down to the Underworld and to the deadly house of Orcus himself. Then hand over the box to Proserpina and say: "Venus asks you to send her a dose of your own beauty, just enough for one short day only. That is because the one she had she has all used up and depleted while taking care of her ailing son." And don't dawdle and come back at once, because I need to anoint myself with it and visit the theatre of the gods.'[19]

6 .17

Then Psyche felt more than ever that her last day had arrived and that the curtain had been drawn, and she realised clearly that she was being pushed towards her immediate death. And how not, since she was forced to travel voluntarily to Tartarus and the shades of the dead, and on her own two feet?[20] No longer did she hesitate, and made for a very high tower, with the intention to throw herself off it,[21] because she thought that like that she could descend to the Underworld straightaway and elegantly. But the tower suddenly broke into speech and said:

'You poor girl, why are you planning to destroy yourself with this jump? And why do you capitulate now so rashly to this very last danger and task of yours? Because once your spirit is separated from your body, you will indeed go straight down to deepest Tartarus, but there is no way that you would be able to return from there!

6 .18

Listen to me! Lacedaemon, the magnificent[22] Achaian city, is not far from here. Search for

Taenarus, which is close to it, but hidden away in an inaccessible area. There is Dis' breathing-vent, and through its gaping doors an impassable path is revealed. Once you have stepped over that threshold and committed yourself to this road, you will reach the palace of Orcus via a direct passage. But you must not advance through these shadowy regions thus far empty-handed; but in each of your hands you must carry cakes made from barley-meal and soaked in honeyed wine, and in your mouth you must hold two small coins.[23] When you have already completed the best part of your death-bringing journey, you will encounter a lame donkey carrying wood with a donkey-driver just like him, who will ask you to hand him some little sticks that had fallen from his load. But you must not make any sound at all and walk past him in silence.[24] Immediately afterwards you will come to the river of the dead, where Charon is in charge, who ferries travellers to the faraway riverbank in his patched-up rowing boat, and he will straightaway demand you pay your toll. Thus we note that even among the dead greed is alive, and that not even Charon, Dis' tax-collector, is so great a god that he would do anything for free. Even a poor man who is dying must find his proper fare money, and if a copper coin doesn't happen to be at hand, he won't be allowed to breathe his last breath. To this filthy old man you will give as his fare one of the coins you are carrying, but arrange it so that he himself should take it out of your mouth with his own hand. Likewise, when you are crossing the slow-moving river, a dead old man floating in it will stretch out his rotting hands and beg you that you should pull him inside the boat. But you must not be moved by an untimely sense of duty.

6 .19

After you have crossed the river and advanced a little further, some old women weavers preparing their loom will ask you to lend them a hand for a little while. But it would be a crime for you to touch it. For all this and many other things will arise for you as Venus' traps, so that you might drop at least one cake from your hands. And do not think lightly of that barley-cake loss: for if you lose either one of them, daylight will be denied to you forever. For there is an enormous dog, and he has three rather large heads, huge and scary, who barks at the dead with thunderous jaws, trying to frighten them, even though he cannot cause them any harm. He always lies in front of the very threshold and the black halls of Proserpina, and guards the insubstantial palace of Dis. Tame him with the offer of one single cake as prey, and you will walk past him easily, and at once into the presence of Proserpina. She will welcome you in a courteous and friendly manner, and try to persuade you to sit down comfortably and share a sumptuous meal with her. But you must sit on the floor, ask for coarse bread, and eat it.[25] After that, announce why you have come, and take what is offered to you. When you return, buy off the dog's wildness with the remaining cake, and after that, once you have given the greedy mariner the coin which you had reserved for him and crossed his river, retrace your earlier steps, and you will return to this band of heavenly stars. But among all these things I advise you to follow this rule especially: you really don't want to open or inspect that box that you carry, or, in fact, to scrutinise too curiously that hidden treasure of divine beauty.'[26]

6
.20

So the future-seeing tower performed the task of prophecy. Psyche did not hesitate and made for Taenarus, and after duly acquiring the coins and cakes, she hurried on her course for the Underworld. She passed the disabled donkey-driver in silence, gave the ferryman her river-fare, disregarded the appeal of the floating corpse, spurned the crafty requests of the textile workers, lulled to sleep the dog's horrible fury with bites of cake, and entered the house of Proserpina. She did not accept the dainty seat and delicious food her hostess offered to her, but sitting down on the floor at her feet and content with rough bread, she passed on Venus' commission. At once the box was filled and closed shut in private, and Psyche picked it up. After closing off the dog's barking with the ruse of the second cake and handing over the remaining coin to the mariner, she ran away from the Underworld quite energetically. When she found and cherished that bright daylight again, although she was in haste to finish her time of service, her mind fell prey to rash curiosity. 'Look,', she said, I am such an idiot to be carrying divine beauty, and not to taste even a teeny tiny drop from it for myself. I might even be able to please my handsome lover like this.'

. . .

6.21

And with these words she opened the box. But there was nothing in there, not any beauty, just sleep, deadly and truly Stygian. As soon as the lid had been removed it overwhelmed her and poured itself over her entire body in a dense languorous cloud. On the very spot and path she was standing on she collapsed, as it took possession of her. And she was lying there motionless, no different than a sleeping corpse.[27]

But Cupid, getting better now that his scar had healed, could bear no longer the long absence of his Psyche, and sneaked out of the highest window of the bedroom in which he had been confined. As his wings had recovered with some rest he flew along much more quickly, and he hurried to his Psyche. After carefully wiping the sleep away and putting it back again in its original place in the box, he roused Psyche with a harmless prick of his arrow. Then he said:

'Look, my poor girl, once again you were ruined because of that very same curiosity. But in the meantime you diligently have to accomplish the mission which has been assigned to you on my mother's command, I will see to everything else.'

With these words her fleeting lover took to his wings. But Psyche swiftly delivered Proserpina's present to Venus.

. . .

6

.22

In the meantime, Cupid was consumed by excessive love and looking sick,[28] and very much in fear of his mother's recent sobriety, he returned to his old tricks. On speedy wings he made it through to the very summit of heaven, knelt before the great Jupiter as a suppliant and pleaded his case. Then Jupiter reached for Cupid's cheeks, moved his hand close to his face, kissed him, and said to him:

'My son and master, even though you have never paid me the honour decreed to me by the agreement of the gods, but instead have wounded this heart of mine, by which the laws of the elements and the paths of the stars are arranged, with constant strikes, and tainted it with frequent incidents of passion on earth, against the laws, especially the Julian one and the one on public order, and have tarnished my reputation and good character with dreadful adulteries by shamefully transforming my fine features into snakes, fires, wild beasts, birds, and farmyard cattle[29] – still, I am mindful of my moderate temper and that you grew up in these arms of mine, and will fulfil what you ask for – but only if you know first how to beware of your rivals, and, secondly if there is right now any girl on earth who stands out in beauty, you must give her to me as compensation for this current favour.'[30]

. . .

6 .23

When he finished speaking, he ordered Mercury to summon all gods immediately to an assembly, and to announce that if anyone was going to be absent from the meeting of the citizens of heaven, they would be liable to a fine of ten thousand sesterces. Because of fear of this the heavenly theatre filled up at once, and towering Jupiter on his splendid throne made the following announcement:

'O gods enrolled in the register of the Muses,[31] you all know very well that I have reared this young man here with my own hands. I have decided that the rash impulses of his early youth have to be reined in somehow. It has been long enough that he has been defamed by daily gossip about his adulteries and all kinds of seductions. We have to remove all opportunity and shackle his youthful extravagance with marriage. He chose a girl and took her maidenhood. Let him have her, let him hold her, let him embrace his Psyche and for ever enjoy his love.'

Then he turned his face to Venus and said: 'Don't be saddened at all, daughter, and don't fear for your great lineage and status because of this matrimony with a mortal. For I will ensure that this marriage is no longer unequal, but legitimate and in accordance with civil law.'

And on the spot he ordered Psyche to be seized by Mercury and to be led into heaven. He offered her a cup of ambrosia and said: 'Take this, Psyche, and become immortal. Never ever will Cupid leave these bonds that bind you together, and this marriage of yours will last for ever.'[32]

6 .24

Instantly a lavish wedding feast was produced. On the couch of honour there reclined the bridegroom, embracing Psyche in his arms. Likewise Jupiter with his Juno, and thereafter all the gods in order. Then a beaker of nectar, which is the wine of the gods, was offered to Jupiter by his own cupbearer, that rustic boy, but Liber served the others. Vulcan cooked the meal, the Horae coloured everything vividly with roses and other flowers; the Graces sprinkled balsam, the Muses, too, made tuneful music in harmony. Apollo sang to his lyre, Venus stepped out to the tune of sweet music and danced beautifully. She had arranged the stage for herself so that the Muses were singing in chorus, a Satyr blew the pipe, and a little Pan played on the shepherd's flute.[33]

And so Psyche was properly given in marriage to Cupid, and when her time came, a girl was born to them both, whom we call Pleasure.[34]

The End

THE WORLD OF APULEIUS

Map of ancient Greece

NOTES: CHAPTER ONE

1. In Greek novels, beautiful girls can commonly be mistaken for goddesses, but Psyche is unique in the sense that she will indeed become a goddess herself at the end of the story. The gesture is one of worship and admiration.

2. Venus was born from the blood of Caelus/Uranus the god of the sky, as it dripped into the sea and combined with it into foam to create the goddess of love. Her Greek name Aphrodite literally means 'born of foam'.

3. Paphos on Cyprus, Cnidos in modern Turkey and the Greek island of Cythera were important ancient sanctuaries of Venus. Neglect of worship of ancient gods was sometimes believed to cause the gods' powers to wane.

4. Venus here sees herself less as the goddess of love, but as the goddess and creator of all nature. Her subsequent tetchiness about her age and appearance (5.29) might explain why she is so irritable here.

5. She recalls the Judgement of Paris, the shepherd, which started the Trojan War. Paris was asked to choose between her, Juno (the goddess of marriage and wife of Zeus-Jupiter) and Athena (the goddess of wisdom) and declare one of them the most beautiful. Enticed by Venus with the promise of the hand of the most beautiful mortal woman alive, he picked her. Paris then abducted Helen from her husband Agamemnon to Troy, which started the Trojan War.

6. Venus' winged and wayward son is none other than Cupid, the young god of Love, armed with his torch and arrows that wound people and thus make them fall in love.

7. Psyche's name is introduced for the first time. In Greek it means both 'soul' and 'butterfly', which allows us to read the story as an allegory of the love of Love and the Soul. In pictures of the couple Cupid often has bird-like wings, whereas Psyche has the wings of a butterfly, though in Apuleius' story she is wingless.

8. Venus returns to be the goddess of the sea, and has a fitting retinue of marine divinities. The image of Venus triumphant was popular with ancient and more recent illustrators. Her retinue consists of the sea god Nereus' fifty daughters, the Nereids; the Roman harbour god Portunus; Salacia, the wife of Neptune, mother of Triton and Roman goddess of the salt waters; Palaemon, a god who saves people lost at sea, rides his dolphins; Tritons, with the body of a man and the tail of a fish generally blow conch shells to stir and calm the sea. Oceanus is

the personification of the world sea that surrounds the earth.

9. 'sick in body, wounded in mind' is a direct quotation of a Latin tragedy (Ennius, *scaen.* 216 Jocelyn) about Medea, but here used deliberately inappropriately for comic effect: in the tragedy, Medea is about to murder her children, but Psyche here is just unhappy that no suitor for her hand appears.

10. Apollo's famous oracle in Didyma near Miletus in modern Turkey.

11. Apollo does a favour to the teller of this Milesian Tale (the author Apuleius), who identifies his novel as a Milesian Tale in *Met.* 1.1. Milesian Tales are short, funny stories often of erotic nature, with unexpected endings. The Greek god speaking in Latin is Apuleius poking gentle fun at the Latin origins of his story, which is likely Apuleius' own invention. Apollo's oracle is in elegiac verse, the metre of, among other things, Latin love poetry.

12. Psyche's marriage recalls that of girls in the ancient world who died before their wedding, and who were therefore said to be married 'to Death'.

13. In Middle Platonism, the philosophical school Apuleius subscribes to, Cupid is sometimes seen as a *daimon*, a divine mediator between humans on earth and the higher-ranked gods in the aether.

14. At first sight, the oracle sounds threatening, but at second glance it alludes to Cupid as the prospective

husband: he has wings and carries torches and arrows (see 4.31). It is a commonplace idea that Cupid is the only thing that Jupiter, the greatest of the gods, and Dis/Hades, the god of the Underworld, fear. See also Jupiter's reaction in 6.22.

15. Styx is a river in the Underworld, see also 6.13.

16. Tibiae are rather loud double-pipe reed instruments used for playing the wedding song, whereas the Lydian mode was considered soft and suitable for mourning.

17. Roman brides wore orange veils, not white.

18. Just like a heroine from Greek tragedy about to be 'married to Death' (e.g. Iphigenia in Euripides, *Iphigenia in Aulis*, or Macaria in Euripides, *Children of Heracles*), Psyche goes to her death willingly.

19. Zephyr is the personification of the gentle West wind.

NOTES: CHAPTER TWO

1. Psyche wakes up in the perfect and idealised landscape of the *locus amoenus* ('pleasant place', a literary topos). The palace may recall sumptuous contemporary Roman villas, but features more extravagant materials betraying its divine origins.

2. Psyche's invisible female servants are one of the most notable parallels to the fairy tale *Beauty and the Beast*, which was inspired by *Cupid and Psyche*.

3. Cupid (whom we guess to be the husband) acts remarkably stealthily. We find out later that he has to hide his relationship with Psyche from his jealous mother, which is one of the reasons for his continued invisibility.

4. Apuleius alludes to a Platonic concept here: the body (*soma*) as the tomb or prison (*sema*) of the immortal soul (Plato, *Gorgias* 492e-493a).

5. Here and elsewhere in the story Apuleius puns on the names of the lovers: Love and Soul.

6. Psyche's made-up description of her husband is inadvertently quite close to the truth.

7. 'By Hercules' is a common interjection, but generally not used by women. The first indication of the sisters' transgressive nature.

8. Romans scoffed at baldness, and the identification with a pumpkin turns the sister's husband into a comic and pathetic character.

9. The sisters are here and elsewhere described with military metaphors, as in laying siege on Psyche.

10. Lamia is a female monster that attacks and devours children; Cupid identifies the sisters as a specifically deadly threat to Psyche and the unborn child.

11. Psyche is with child, and should know from what her husband tells her here that she is married to a god. The threat that the child might be born human does not come to pass, as at the moment of her daughter's birth Psyche has already become a goddess herself.

12. Furies are the restless goddesses of vengeance, often pictured with snakes in their hair.

13. Sirens are monstrous birds with human faces. Their songs are seductive and deceitful.

14. The sisters guess correctly the identity of Psyche's husband, whereas 'simple Psyche' remains oblivious.

15. In Greek tragedy, women hanging themselves is metaphorically connected to anxieties about marriage and childbirth; this is an indication of the sisters' true motives.

16. Psyche knows that her husband has human features, she can feel them (5.13), but she still believes her sisters that her husband is a snake. The sisters must have suggested that the husband is a shape-shifter, able to take on human or serpentine form at will. In the frame narrative, the narrator of the novel encounters just such a shape-shifter, who in his snake form devours a young man (*Met.* 8.19-21). The idea of Cupid as a snake-like monster is ancient, see e.g. the poet Sappho's famous description of Love as a 'bitter-sweet, unmoveable creeping creature' (130 Lobel-Page).

17. Apollo's Pythian oracle is in Delphi, which is not the one consulted by Psyche's father. The sisters here allude to Apollo as the slayer of the Python, a dangerous mythological snake which the god killed near Delphi.

18. On Furies see 5.11; here Psyche is thinking about committing a crime that could result in her being persecuted by the Furies, but the phrase also recalls her sisters, who are making her do it.

19. Ambrosia is the food and cosmetic of the gods, which gives them immortality.

20. This description echoes Plato's philosophical dialogue *Phaedrus* 248c where it is explained that souls too heavy with absentmindedness and evilness lose their wings and fall to earth. Apuleius was a Platonic philosopher. It is

warmly discussed among scholars whether this passage turns the whole of the story of *Cupid and Psyche* into a Platonic allegory of Love and the Soul, or whether it is merely a playful literary allusion.

21. The river is the first of many inanimate objects that will now help Psyche in her perils, in the suspicion, it seems, that Cupid has not completely washed his hands of Psyche despite what he had said.

22. Pan is the rustic god of goatherds and shepherds, here embracing Echo, his beloved nymph. He has goat legs and horns, and often plays the pan pipe to create 'panic', but here becomes a gentle love counsellor and consoler for Psyche's loneliness and pain. His love for Echo is often represented as only one-sided, but here is mutual, to make Pan an appropriately successful advisor in terms of love.

23. Psyche claims here that Cupid has divorced her, by using the common Roman divorce formula. The proposed marriage to the sister, she says, will be the most solemn marriage ceremony possible in Roman law, the *confarreatio*, which requires ten witnesses and is thought to be blessed by Jupiter himself.

24. Although Psyche's untruths play a part in her sisters' deaths, the main blame here lies with the sister: she left her own husband without an appropriate divorce, and ignored the fact that Zephyr was not present near the rock when she jumped.

25. Normally, chatty birds betraying gods' secrets in

mythology tend to be ravens or crows; this seagull is unique in this role.

26. The entourage Venus suspects of seducing Cupid consists of minor goddesses: Nymphs (goddesses of nature), Horae (goddesses in charge of time), the nine Muses (goddesses of art), and the Graces (goddesses of beauty and abundance).

27. It is quite unclear in mythology who Cupid's father is, already in antiquity, which adds to the funny nature of this outburst. But see the next note.

28. Cupid's stepfather here is the god of War, Mars/Ares. Technically, Venus is married to Vulcan, the god of fire, but famously committed adultery with Mars. In Roman mythology, the pairing of Venus and Mars as a couple is much more common because both gods have connections with the founding of Rome. Still, this well-known ambiguity about their relationship gives Venus' domestic quarrel a humorous twist.

29. Sobriety or Temperance is an ad hoc personification of one of Venus' enemies. Personifications like this, almost always female, are a sign of the story's Roman nature.

30. Nectar, together with ambrosia (see on 5.22), is the drink of the gods.

31. Ceres (see on 6.2) and Juno (see on 6.4) are worthy goddesses here solicitously (and comically) reacting to Venus' outburst.

NOTES: CHAPTER THREE

1. Psyche approaches the temple of Ceres; as the goddess of agriculture, she has wheatsheaves, barley and agricultural tools decorating her temple.

2. Psyche's prayer to Ceres follows the proper rules of prayer in antiquity. She lists, among other things, the goddess' divine properties: Ceres/Demeter is the goddess of harvest, but also oversees (in Eleusis near Athens) the Eleusinian mystery cult dedicated to her, where secret rituals took place, possibly involving the basket mentioned here. The abduction in Sicily alludes to her daughter Proserpina/Persephone, who was kidnapped by Dis/Hades the god of the Underworld who made her his wife. Ceres searched for her daughter far and wide, and in the end Proserpina was allowed to spend half the year with her mother above, and half a year below ground with her husband in the Underworld. The goddesses' chthonic nature (i.e. their links with the divinities of the

Underworld) is exemplified by Ceres' chariot pulled by snakes.

3. The temple belongs to Juno, the sister and wife of Jupiter, here evoked as the god of thunder. Psyche's prayer is again following the traditional prayer formula. The island of Samos, Carthage in North Africa (where Juno is identified with the Phoenician goddess Tanit) and Argos on the banks of the River Inachos on the Peloponnese contain famous sanctuaries of Juno. Zygia is a cult title of Juno in her role as the goddess of marriage, and Lucina as the goddess of childbirth – both specialities are important for Psyche now. Juno Sospita ('Saviour') is yet another cult title, linked especially with the city of Lanuvium in Italy. Psyche assures Juno that she knows she is worshipped all over the known ancient world, and in many different aspects. As she is the mother of Mars (as well as of Venus' 'proper' husband Vulcan/Hephaistos; see on 5.31), she is doubly Venus' mother-in-law.

4. Now it is made clear that the skilful god Vulcan, not Mars, is Venus' husband, and had given her a carefully carved divine chariot as a wedding present. Doves are sacred to Venus and occasionally pull her chariot, along with other birds, such as sparrows, which here form the goddess' escort.

5. Caelus/Uranus is Venus' father (see 4.28).

6. Mercury is the messenger god, especially for Jupiter, who here agrees by nodding approval to Venus' borrowing him. Mercury was born on Mount Cyllene in Arcadia as the son of Jupiter and Maia, and therefore is,

strictly speaking, not Venus' brother, unless a variant genealogy is assumed for her, in which she is the daughter of Zeus/Jupiter and Dione. Apuleius plays with both family trees, and Venus is clearly the daughter of Jupiter at 6.23.

7. Venus uses Mercury as a town-crier searching for her runaway slave girl, continuing Psyche's social degradation from princess which started in 5.31. The scene echoes a humorous poem by the Hellenistic Greek poet Moschus, where Eros/Cupid is the runaway being searched (Eros the Runaway). The *metae Murtiae* or Murcian turning points were the turning-posts in the Circus Maximus in Rome, near the temple of Venus Murcia, a localised version of the goddess.

8. Consuetudo, 'Familiarisation' or 'Habit', is a unique personification here as Venus' servant, possibly an echo of the proverbial idea that habitual contact might lead to love ('Familiarisation furthers love') see 5.4 for this concept in action.

9. Orcus is a specifically Roman term for the realm of the dead.

10. Two further abstractions are introduced for the first time in Latin literature as Venus' maid servants: Sollicitudo ('Worry') and Tristities ('Sadness') although similar abstracts appear in Greek and Roman comedy in lists of ad hoc abstract deities/emotions related to love.

11. Some ancient gemstones show a girl with butterfly wings being tortured, at times by a winged Cupid,

although the relationship between these stones and Apuleius' story is unclear.

12. Roman laws prohibited marriage between slaves and freeborn Romans. Furthermore, Venus' claim that Cupid's marriage to Psyche is invalid, because it took place in a country villa without witnesses and the father's consent echoes in some respects Apuleius' own marriage to his wife Pudentilla, whom he married in the countryside, and allegedly without her family's permission.

13. Venus' first task for Psyche of sorting out grains is quite possibly the source of the fairy tale of Cinderella, but with ants instead of mice or doves.

14. 'All-mother' is a typical epithet for Earth, the goddess Terra.

15. Venus' second task involves the collecting of golden wool from a flock of unguarded golden sheep. It echoes the myth of the Golden Fleece, which Jason and the Argonauts are sent to collect under dangerous and heroic circumstances.

16. A reed tells Psyche the truth, under divine influence – possibly a sign that Cupid helps Psyche behind the scenes here and elsewhere.

17. Venus' third task asks Psyche to gather water from the spring that feeds two of the Underworld's rivers, Styx and Cocytus, and thus approach, but not quite yet enter, the Underworld. Dragons that never sleep guard ancient treasures that need to be retrieved as part of a hero's quest,

like the Golden Fleece in the story of the Argonauts, or the golden apples of the Hesperides, which form one of Hercules' labours.

18. After the water warns Psyche away, another supernatural helper appears. Jupiter's eagle, who had previously kidnapped the Trojan prince Ganymede from Phrygia in modern Turkey to become the gods' cup bearer (see 6.24), now comes to Psyche's aid.

19. Venus' fourth and final task involves a katabasis, a descent into the Underworld, which is a common theme in epic (e.g. the heroes Odysseus and Aeneas need to go to the Underworld to find out about their future fate). Psyche's task is more feminine, to get a beauty cream from Proserpina, the goddess of the Underworld (see on 6.2).

20. Tartarus is the deepest place of the Underworld where evil-doers are punished after death.

21. Psyche plans to jump off a tower to kill herself in order to reach the it, and is again stopped by a sentient thing, as the tower tells her an easier way to reach the realm of the dead and to stay alive. The scene is based on a Greek Old Comedy, Aristophanes' *Frogs* 117-133, where the god of wine and theatre Dionysus/Bacchus also needs to go on a quest to the Underworld, to retrieve his favourite tragic poet who has recently died.

22. Lacedaemon, i.e. Sparta, is situated in Achaia in the South of the Peleponnese. Taenaros was one of its nearby promontories (today Cape Matapan), and believed in

antiquity to be an entrance to the Underworld. For Dis/Hades and Orcus see on 4.33 and 6.8.

23. Two barley cakes with honey and coins are needed to pacify the three-headed dog guarding the Underworld, Cerberus, and to pay Charon the ferryman to cross the river Styx. Two of each are needed since she needs to go back up as well as down to the Underworld. The dead were commonly buried with a coin placed in their mouth for Charon.

24. The command of silence and haste associates Psyche's task with mystery cult initiations, during which the initiands had to undergo certain tasks in silence; the tasks echo the journeys into the Underworld by epic heroes, although the characters Psyche is to encounter are unique to her own journey, e.g. talking to or helping the old man with his donkey, the old man asking to be taken on board the boat, or the old textile workers in 6.19, would require Psyche to drop her barley cakes or coins, and therefore condemn her to staying in the Underworld.

25. Proserpina herself was tempted to eat in the Underworld by her abductor Dis/Hades, and as she ate some pomegranate seeds, she was obliged to stay for some months of the year (which explains winter in mythological terms). Psyche is warned not to touch and eat anything fancy, so that she can return to earth. The tower's instruction to consume merely some coarse bread while sitting on the ground like a beggar strikes a somewhat unusual and homely compromise between the required positive response to the goddess' offer of

hospitality and the need to avoid eating the food of the dead.

26. The divine taboo not to look at the contents of Proserpina's box echoes Cupid's taboo not to look at him.

27. The beauty of the goddess of the realm of the dead is, unsurprisingly, deathlike sleep. Psyche's character has not changed – she is as brave, naïve and curious now as she was at the beginning of her story.

28. Cupid displays some signs of love sickness, believed to be a real disease in the ancient world.

29. Jupiter, not the most faithful of gods, blames Cupid for his affairs with human women, for which he often disguised himself as an animal in order to seduce his human lovers. It is especially Cupid's fault, he claims, that he has broken the Julian marriage laws introduced by the Roman emperor Augustus, which encouraged marriage and childbearing, and discouraged adultery.

30. Jupiter's reward for helping Cupid is to be able to meet even more beautiful mortal women with his assistance, clearly contradicting his previous declarations of modesty and morality.

31. The album of the Muses is an allusion to the register of senators in Rome, and the council of the gods humorously echoes an assembly of the Roman senate.

32. By making Psyche immortal with a drink of ambrosia, Jupiter ensures the marriage of Cupid and Psyche is between equals in accordance with Roman law, where e.g.

the marriage between a freeborn person and a slave (as Venus claimed Psyche to be earlier) is not permitted.

33. The divine wedding party reunites the whole pantheon: Ganymede (see on 6.15) and Bacchus the god of wine (Apuleius always uses the Latin form Liber) serve the drinks, Vulcan the god of fire prepares the food, the goddesses of Venus' entourage in 5.28 again form a festive group. Apollo the god of music plays on his lyre as usual, and Venus, apparently reconciled to the marriage, dances for everyone. A goat- legged Satyr and a little Pan (i.e. not the rather elderly Pan who previously gave advice to Psyche in 5.25, but a minor goat-herding god) play the tibiae and pan-pipes.

34. The name of the daughter, Pleasure, is symbolic for the joy any reader of the story of Cupid and Psyche feels.

Apuleius: Metamorphoses Book I (Aris & Phillips Classical Texts, Oxford 2013)

Apuleius and Drama: The Ass on Stage (Oxford Classical Monographs, Oxford 2006)